— MONSTER WARS —
ZOMBIES VS.
MUMMIES

CLASH OF THE LIVING DEAD

by Michael O'Hearn

Consultant:
Michael Delahoyde, PhD
Washington State University
Pullman, Washington

CAPSTONE PRESS
a capstone imprint

Edge Books are published by Capstone Press,
151 Good Counsel Drive, P.O. Box 669, Mankato, Minnesota 56002.
www.capstonepub.com

 Books published by Capstone Press are manufactured with paper
containing at least 10 percent post-consumer waste.

Library of Congress Cataloging-in-Publication Data
O'Hearn, Michael, 1972–
    Zombies vs. mummies : clash of the living dead / by Michael O'Hearn.
    p. cm.—(Edge books. Monster wars)
    Summary: "Describes the features and abilities of zombies and mummies and
how they may battle each other in a fight"—Provided by publisher.
    Includes bibliographical references and index.
    ISBN 978-1-4296-6520-9 (library binding)
    ISBN 978-1-4296-7267-2 (paperback)
    1. Zombies—Juvenile literature. 2. Mummies—Juvenile literature.
I. Title. II. Series.
BF1556.O55 2012
398'.45—dc22   2011003785

Editorial Credits
Aaron Sautter, editor; Tracy Davies, designer; Eric Gohl, media researcher;
        Eric Manske, production specialist

Illustrations
Patricia Moffett

Photo Credits
Alamy/AF Archive, 9 (bottom), 17 (bottom); Doug Steley A, 6 (right);
    Photos 12, 10, 13
BigStockPhoto.com/John Salandiak, 6 (left); Szabo Balazs, 5 (bottom)
Getty Images Inc./Pictorial Parade, 14
Kobal Collection/Hammer, 15; Universal, 12
Mary Evans Picture Library/Ronald Grant Archive, 11; Amblin
    Entertainment, 5 (top)
Newscom/Album/Universal Pictures, 9 (top), 17 (top), 19 (left);
    Getty Images/AFP/Tim Sloan, 19 (right)
Shutterstock/Danomyte (mummy silhouette); Yuran (zombie silhouette)

Printed in the United States of America in Stevens Point, Wisconsin.

032011   006111WZF11

TABLE OF CONTENTS

Chapter 1 — Welcome to Monsters Wars! 4

Chapter 2 — The Frightening Truth:

Zombie vs. Mummy 6

Special Powers 8

Intelligence 10

Strength.................................. 12

Speed 14

Weaknesses 16

Chapter 3 — Get Ready to Rumble! 18

Chapter 4 — Clash of the Undead 20

Glossary 30

Read More 31

Internet Sites 31

Index... 32

WELCOME TO MONSTER WARS!

It's past midnight. The night is dark. Shadows creep across your bedroom wall. You swear they form a slit-eyed face. Floorboards creak. Trees outside your window groan. It's nothing, you tell yourself. But you lie awake … watching … listening … waiting. You can't help but think a terrifying monster is hiding in your closet.

In these pages, you'll learn the strengths and weaknesses of zombies and mummies. And you'll see them battle each other head to head. Will the zombies unravel the mummy when he climbs from his **tomb**? Or will the mummy unleash his revenge and send the walking dead back to the grave?

Are monsters real? No. But be ready for a creepy nighttime battle.

tomb — a grave or room that holds a dead body

THE FRIGHTENING TRUTH:

ZOMBIE VS. MUMMY

Ancient Egyptians mummified their dead. They removed a dead body's organs, except the heart. The body was then dried out with a type of salt called natron. Finally, the body was wrapped in linen cloth. The ancient Egyptians believed that preserving bodies in this way helped the dead live again in the afterlife.

In movies and stories about mummies, **curses** and spells bring a mummy back to life. These mummies usually turn monstrous. They seek revenge on anyone who disturbs their tombs or gets in their way.

Zombies are also popular undead creatures in stories and movies. Zombies are walking corpses that have clawed their way out of their graves. A deadly virus often turns people into flesh-eating zombies. Each new zombie spreads the sickness, which creates even more zombies. Sometimes poisonous sludge or **radiation** causes bodies to rise from the grave. Before long, the walking dead surround the living—and they're hungry for human flesh!

But which of these monsters is more dangerous? Read on to learn their undeadly secrets!

curse — an evil spell meant to harm someone
radiation — rays of energy given off by certain elements

SPECIAL POWERS

Mummies can return to life when someone breaks into their tomb and reads an evil spell. The spell may also give the mummy powerful magic. Some mummies can control a person's mind or attack their enemies from far away. Sometimes, as they grow in power, they may look less like a mummy and more like a person. With a renewed body, they can move more easily among the living.

Zombies don't have magic. But their power is just as deadly. With just one bite, zombies can turn the living into the undead. If a zombie bites someone, that person becomes infected with the zombie sickness. If the person escapes without being eaten, the sickness will eventually kill him. After he dies, he'll rise again as a new flesh-eating zombie.

MUMMY magical abilities
★★★★

ZOMBIE deadly, infectious bite
★★★

FRIGHTFUL FACT

In some movies, mummies have the power to control the wind and create desert sands.

INTELLIGENCE

MUMMY clever and smart
★ ★ ★

ZOMBIE dim-witted undead
★

Zombies often like to eat brains. But the brains in their own heads aren't very useful. Zombies can't think. They have only a dull **instinct** to eat fresh meat. They're always hungry, and they continually wander looking for food. But they're not smart enough to look for places that have plenty of people to eat.

Mummies have no brains in their heads. But they're still smart. Mummies know what they want. They usually want to find a special magic book or treasure. And they won't think twice about killing someone to get it. In this battle of the brain-eater versus the brainless, the mummy has a definite advantage in smarts.

FRIGHTFUL FACT

Before wrapping a dead body, the ancient Egyptians used a hook to pull the brain out through the nose.

instinct — behavior that is natural

STRENGTH

MUMMY magical power
★ ★ ★ ★

ZOMBIE average muscles
★ ★

Mummies are made to live forever in the afterlife. When they come back from the dead, they are magically strong. A mummy can lift a grown man by the neck and fling him across the room. Or he can crush a person's skull with his hands. A mummy has plenty of strength to defend himself from a pack of hungry zombies.

Shuffling undead zombies are only as strong as when they were alive. Their flesh also **decays**, which makes them weaker over time. When their bodies are damaged, they don't heal. But zombies do have one advantage. They can't feel pain. They just keep attacking until they are dead—again!

FRIGHTFUL FACT

Zombie movies often center on an end-of-the-world situation. In several films, scientists or the government accidentally create a sickness that causes an outbreak of the walking dead.

decay — to break down or rot

SPEED

MUMMY stiff and very sluggish
★

ZOMBIE slow, shuffling feet
★★

Zombies usually move slowly. They stagger and drag their feet. They may have broken bones, ripped flesh, and torn muscles. Zombies aren't likely to run down their victims. But when there are enough zombies, they can surround and trap victims, cutting off their escape.

Mummies move even more slowly than zombies. A mummy's body is usually thousands of years old. It's stiff and dried out, and its body is wrapped tightly in cloth from head to toe. Rather than chase after people, mummies tend to surprise their victims and grab them from the shadows.

FRIGHTFUL FACT

Mummies have been found in countries around the world including Chile, Denmark, Peru, China, and Japan.

WEAKNESSES

Mummies are usually brought to life by a curse that someone reads from a scroll. The scroll gives the mummy its power. Sometimes if the scroll is destroyed, the mummy dies. But the tried-and-true way to kill a mummy is with fire. Wrapped in so much dried-out cloth, mummies are like a match just waiting to be lit.

Destroy a zombie's brain and you kill the zombie. Whether it's a bullet or a blow to the head, zombies are fairly easy to kill. The problem is finding and killing all of them. As zombies spread their sickness, they multiply quickly. It's rare to find only a few zombies. Where there is one zombie, you're likely to find many of them.

MUMMY vulnerable to fire
★★★

ZOMBIE unprotected brains
★★

FRIGHTFUL FACT

Mummies are often afraid of cats in movies and stories. Cats were considered holy and were worshipped in ancient Egypt. Mummies are evil monsters, so cats are their natural enemy.

3

GET READY TO RUMBLE!

You'll hear their slow, staggering footsteps long before you see these undead foes clash. Can a zombie spread its sickness to a long-dead mummy? Will the mummy's strength and magic overcome a zombie attack? There are more questions than answers as this battle begins. But one thing is certain—one of these monsters will return to the grave. The other will keep bringing terror to all who cross its path.

Hide under the bed if you must, but don't stop reading. You have a graveyard seat for this monstrous battle. It's a clash of the living dead!

MUMMY

	SPECIAL POWERS	INTELLIGENCE	STRENGTH	SPEED	WEAKNESSES
MUMMY	★★★★	★★★	★★★★	★	★★★
ZOMBIE	★★★	★	★★	★★	★★

ZOMBIE

ONE LAST THING ...

The following fight is based on legends and stories. Walking undead zombies aren't real at all. Mummies are real, but they don't come back to life. However, you can still use your imagination. So dim the lights, turn the page, and get ready to be scared stiff!

CLASH OF THE UNDEAD

★ ★ ★ ★ ★ ★

The mummy slowly curls his fingers into a fist. He pounds his wrapped knuckles against the lid of the crate that holds him. The wood bends, then cracks, and finally bursts apart. The mummy sits straight up.

A dozen lightbulbs hang from the ceiling. They sway and light the room in a dim, shifting glow. The mummy stands stiffly. Strips of cloth hang from his body. He kicks away the broken pieces of his crate and stumbles toward a staircase.

His knees barely bend as he lumbers forward. Suddenly, a pale, limping zombie appears on the stairway.

The zombie trips and falls down the last few steps. His face is bruised and his nose is bent. He moans and sniffs the air. On his knees, he stares hungrily at the mummy.

The mummy stomps forward as the zombie climbs to its feet. The zombie stumbles toward the mummy, reaching out to grab his next victim. The monster grabs the mummy's arm and bites down with decaying teeth.

The mummy groans. He raises his arm and lifts the zombie off the ground. The zombie bites down harder. Suddenly, one rotted tooth snaps. Then a mouthful of blackened, yellow teeth break loose and rain to the floor. The zombie drops in a heap beside them.

The mummy reaches down and grabs the undead zombie. He flips the monster upside down and bashes it into a nearby crate up to its waist. Unable to attack, the stuck zombie kicks his legs slowly in the air.

The mummy climbs the stairs and reaches the deck of a ship. High above the deck, black smoke streams from a large smokestack. Thick clouds cover the moon. The night sky is dim.

Skinny zombies dressed like sailors wander the deck aimlessly. The mummy stares at the strange creatures. One zombie chews on some rope tied to a lifeboat. Another bumps against a closed door trying to walk forward. The ship presses on through the sea.

The zombies moan and stare blankly. They stagger toward the mummy. They claw at him and snap their jaws. One zombie grabs the mummy's cloth wrapping and tugs loose a strip of fabric. The mummy swats the tall, pale monster. He knocks the flesh-eater down, but the zombie holds tightly to the cloth.

The mummy bends stiffly and grabs his enemy by the neck. He lifts the creature high and throws it over the side of the ship. The zombie splashes into the water and sinks.

Now the mummy stands at the edge of the deck. A long piece of cloth drags behind him. Starving zombies crowd around him, grabbing and biting. The mummy raises his hand. Suddenly, a wall of sand magically appears and blasts across the deck. A dozen of the walking dead are swept off the ship and into the sea.

Still more zombies come. The mummy grabs one undead monster by the neck and tosses it overboard. He picks up another zombie and throws it at some other flesh-eaters. Six of the walking dead are knocked to the ship's deck.

But still more of the monsters appear. Zombies stumble down from upper decks. They limp out of doorways. They tumble out of lifeboats. The frenzied creatures swarm the mummy and overwhelm him. They bite down on the mummy's arms, shoulders, ankles, and neck.

The zombies rip off the mummy's wrappings until they reach the dried flesh beneath. They soon crawl over the mummy's twice-dead body. They feast until only the mummy's shredded wrappings remain.

GLOSSARY

corpse (KORPS)—a dead body

curse (KURS)—an evil spell meant to harm someone

decay (di-KAY)—to break down or rot

infect (in-FEKT)—to transmit a disease by introducing germs

instinct (IN-stingkt)—behavior that is natural rather than learned

organ (OR-guhn)—a part of the body that does a certain job, such as the brain, heart, or lungs

radiation (ray-dee-AY-shuhn)—rays of energy given off by certain elements

tomb (TOOM)—a grave, room, or building that holds a dead body

virus (VYE-ruhss)—a tiny germ that infects living things and can cause disease

READ MORE

Hamilton, S. L. *Zombies*. Xtreme Monsters. Edina, Minn.: ABDO Pub. Company, 2011.

MacDonald, Fiona. *The Ancient Egyptians: Dress, Eat, Write, and Play Just Like the Egyptians*. Hands-on History. New York: Crabtree Pub., 2008.

Putnam, James. *Mummy*. Eyewitness Books. London; New York: DK Pub., 2009.

INTERNET SITES

FactHound offers a safe, fun way to find Internet sites related to this book. All of the sites on FactHound have been researched by our staff.

Here's all you do:

Visit *www.facthound.com*

Type in this code: 9781429665209

 Check out projects, games and lots more at
www.capstonekids.com

INDEX

ancient Egyptians, 7, 11

mummies
    attack style of, 4, 8, 15, 22,
        26, 28
    creation of, 8, 16
    and curses, 7, 16
    intelligence of, 11
    locations of, 15
    and magic spells, 7, 8, 18
    powers of, 8, 9, 26
    revenge of, 4, 7
    speed of, 15, 18, 20
    strength of, 12, 18, 20,
        22, 26, 28
    weaknesses of, 16, 17
mummification, 7, 11

zombies
    attack style of, 4, 8, 14, 22,
        26, 28
    creation of, 7, 8, 13
    hunger of, 7, 10, 22, 25, 26
    intelligence of, 10, 25
    and radiation, 7
    speed of, 14, 18, 22, 25,
        26, 28
    strength of, 13
    and viruses, 7, 8, 16, 18
    weaknesses of, 16